Inside out

A collection of poems by Alex Rasmussen

This book is dedicated to the miles, places, conversations, and faces.

They have a wonderful way
of shaping a person.

Por Siempre

All-you-can-eat mango chicken.
Rice and beans, deep-fried plantains.
Only two hundred pesos.

Pinch me.

The mojitos are made fresh.
After each sip, I pick mint from my teeth.

The Cuban band is at it again,
jamming their afternoon set in front of an open window.
The vast blue Pacific smiles from behind the bass player,
the conga man.
The palm trees have forgotten to bring their IDs,
so they watch the show from outside.

A two-story place with white walls,
black marker scrawled across every inch,
forty years of names, dates, and concise declarations.
Some of love.
Many of love, in a place like this.

Maria y Carlos, por siempre.

Even the white, cylindrical lamp shades that dangle above
the bar have been marked by those brave enough to balance
atop the wobbly stools.
After a few of these mojitos,
that could prove quite the feat.

Out of the sunlight,
a man and girl strut through the door;
he leads the way.
Hand in hand, they find a table and sit down.

My buddy looks at the girl,
then at the man.

"Guy must be loaded," my buddy says.
I consider the girl. Early twenties,
a fair-faced Latina with large, curious eyes and a confident
glow, seated with provocative poise across from a man who
looks as though he could be her grandfather.
"Yeah," I agree.
"Looks about right."

There is a strange mechanical groan,
and the middle of the room begins to glow.
The light expands, growing brighter.
My buddy and I look up.
The roof is sliding apart,
the sky's blue eye opening above us.

We are now drinking outside.

I order another plate of mango chicken,
another mojito.

Periodically, I steal glances at the young beauty as she
converses enthusiastically with the man across from her.

Crimson lips open wide when she laughs.

Beyond the girl's reaction to this man,
all I can see of him is the back of his graying head,
bobbing slightly as he continues to make her smile.

Suddenly, the band kicks into an up-tempo tune, and the
man and girl lean forward in mutual recognition of the song.
He takes her hand, and they stand.
As soon as they clear the table,
he spins her atop the black and white tile.

She glides gracefully in thick heels.
Their bodies move fluidly to the island sound,
elbows bent, hips swaying,
faces wearing matching looks of supreme contentment.

Synchronized sensuality.

With both hands, he pulls her close.
She looks up at him, into him,

loses herself,

and then I understand.

Force

It's alive.
If you open your ears, it will call to you:

The voice of the one thing you desire,
the single word you'd like to say,
the only thing you'd choose to do.

Say it.
Do it.

And, out of respect,
the force will lead you to extraordinary places,
show you scenes you never thought possible.

You see,
it rewards those brave enough to live from the inside out.

We have an interesting relationship,
this power and I.
It has been known to dance with me one day,
only to leave me behind the next.

I can't blame it, though.

That force sees through me,
and it has no tolerance for cowardice or dishonesty.

So, in times when I am weak,
the force leaves me to ponder and evolve,

Knowing that its time would be best spent
in the company of those living in the light,
rather than wasted on some fool who hides in safe shadows.

Elastic Elana

The first time she showed me one of her paintings—
splashed onto the paper in short bursts of whisky madness—
I tried to find something that I liked about it
"Those colors you've chosen really go well together."

I wasn't lying.
But I also didn't tell her that I thought she'd never sell the
piece, as she was planning to.

Who was I to put a price on her art, though?
Who was I to say that someone wouldn't see what she saw?

I ordered another beer.
She, another whisky.
Then, with one earbud blasting her favorite band—the other
ear was left alone, so our conversation could continue—she
proceeded to dip the paintbrush in blue before slashing it,
like a swashbuckler, across the defenseless paper.
After the strike, Elana immediately drew back,
rubbing her chin and considering the effect of her blow.
Without warning, she attacked again.
And again.

After reloading her brush with paint,
Elana took a sip while contemplating her next move.
Then, entertaining a sudden burst of inspiration,
she slammed the glass down and lashed out.

Her passion fascinated me, though the work itself did not.
Elana seemed to harbor emotions begging for some outlet,
but as far as I could tell these were simply spewed onto the
page without any clarity or form.
This may have been exactly what Elana was after,
exactly what she was feeling—some internal whirlwind;
but her storm failed to move anything inside me.

"I think," Elana spoke between brushstrokes,

"you have to erase your ego.
Allow the force to flow through you. Be an open channel."
Elana rested a palm on her cheek, eyes wide,
staring at the paper while searching for her next words.
She glanced at me, quickly, as if some invisible entity had
jerked her head my direction.
Elana pointed a finger.
"If the ego blocks that channel, you get nothing."
She went back to painting, and I sipped my beer, listening.

"That's why all those guys were all so fucked up.
'Cause they were vulnerable.
Everything affected them."
Elana laid her brush on a paint-stained napkin before
grabbing another brush from the cup in front of her.
She dipped the new brush in red and continued to speak as
she worked.

"The way I see it, you have to be elastic.
Let life *move* you, bend you. Affect you.
Don't be a brick wall. A brick wall won't create shit,
'cause nothing moves the wall. Nothing affects it.
Be elastic, like a rubber band or something. You know,
something pulls at that, and it just *beeeends* back, and the
further it bends, the more force there is when it *shoots* the
other direction!"

When Elana said "shoots," she swung the paintbrush in front
of her and threw a streak of red across the face of the
bartender, who was muddling a mojito.

Elana was asked to leave.

That was the first time I'd met Elana, 6 months ago,
and I had the pleasure of running into her again today.
Same bar, same stool.
Same single earbud,
paint supplies scattered across the counter in front of her.

Her arms moved frantically, attached to a body that swayed
slowly like a patient snake.
A thoughtful hand found her chin.

"Whatcha working on?" I asked while hanging my coat on a
hook below the bar.
"Well," she spoke without looking up from her work.
"I've recently taken over a small country."
She turned to face me, squinting her eyes and whispering
with a hand cupped around her mouth.
"I make all the citizens wear underwear on their heads.
And they can only wash 'em once every two weeks."
Elana removed her hand and snickered to herself.
I laughed and pointed to the painting in progress.
"I mean, what's this?"
"Oh, this!"
Elana set her brush down to grab the paper with both hands.
She then held the fresh creation an inch from my face,
nearly smearing wet paint across my nose.
I leaned back to get a better look.

Two human figures—painted using black and white—sat
facing each other inside a bubble at the center of the paper.
Outside the bubble, multi-colored streaks tangled angrily,
attacking from every angle and appearing determined to
penetrate the peace of the couple's cocoon.

I peered beyond the painting to its creator who had, for the
moment, traded an air of unshakable confidence for some
nervous uncertainty.

"What do you think?" she asked bashfully.

I scanned the work once more before looking to her.
Then, happy to tell the wholehearted truth,
I answered.

"I love it."

Thing

I shot upright in bed.
Darkness.

I couldn't see the Thing.
But I could feel its presence.

My eyes adjusted to the low light,
yet I still couldn't make out any figure.

It was watching me, though.
I knew it.

I turned toward the window and pried the plastic slats apart
with my little fingers,
allowing me a glimpse of the road below.

Cars were parked along a silent street.
2 AM drizzle.
Bare branches swayed slowly in the winter wind.
A trash can lay on its side,
contents vomited onto the pavement.

A plastic bag blew lazily down the sidewalk,
urban tumbleweed.

There it was:
A shadow standing beneath the streetlight.

My stomach tightened in one horrible spasm.

A man.
Maybe.

The Thing didn't move.
It just watched.

I pulled my fingers from the blinds.

The slats snapped shut.

I closed my eyes and prayed. To something.
Anything.
My grandparents had told me about Jesus, so I chose him.
That was supposed to help.

When I opened the blinds again, the Thing was still there.
Shadow standing,
watching.

It knew me.
Knew everything about me.

It knew that my Father wasn't home to protect me.

The Thing was waiting for me to fall asleep.
Then it would make its move.

If I stayed awake, I would stay safe.

I laid back down and stared at the ceiling,
which began to undulate in creamy waves.

When I became bored of this,
I sat up and observed the shadows in the corners of the room
that would dance and grow and shrink.

Heavy footsteps stomped up the front stairs.

My body became rigid.
I couldn't move. No breath.

There was a growling mumble.

The front door opened.
Slammed shut!
A terrible voice barked some word I couldn't understand.

The Thing lumbered up the stairs,
dragged a shoulder against the hallway wall.

It was coming toward my room.

I leapt out of bed and tiptoed across the carpet
toward the closet.
I slid the door open and hid inside
behind the hanging clothes.

It won't find me here.

The Thing moved down the hall,
steel feet stamping closer.
Just outside my door.

I closed my eyes and prayed. To something.
Anything.
My grandparents had told me about Jesus, so I chose him.

And,
thanks to him,

The Thing went into my Father's room and left me alone.

*

She's yours now
But she was once mine

Soon she will be his
Maybe hers

After that she will belong
To the earth
And the stars
And the sky

Again

And one day you will realize
That you never had her
Because you never could

She is everything
And so are you

And for a sweet moment
A blink in the eyes of eternity
You both recognized this truth

Reminded each other of your power
Your divinity

And then the moment was done

But your eyes remained open

<u>Two Truths</u>

Without curiosity
We are dead

Without beer
I am thirsty

Front Lines

It hurts, doesn't it?
When you say, "Hello,"
and instead of responding,
they quickly avert their fearful eyes.

It hurts, doesn't it?
When they say that your clothes,
the way you think,
and the way you speak
are strange.

It stings,
but somehow
you enjoy it.
Because it means you aren't like them.

And you never will be.

It hurts, doesn't it?
When you tell them something heartfelt,
something important,
and they don't even look up from their phones.

It hurts, doesn't it?
When they lie to you,
disrespect your time,
and play games with you.

They lead you on
because they want the attention,
but they're too scared to be vulnerable,
to connect.

It hurts, doesn't it?
Feeling like you're too small
to have a significant impact
on this often twisted world,

feeling no more influential than a grain of sand.

It hurts, doesn't it?
Fighting day after day
against a culture that wants to shape you.

You that is honest.
You that is radiant.
You that is brave and bold and beautiful.
Yes.
It hurts.

And I imagine it will always hurt

striving to be open-minded,
unique,
courageous,
hopeful,
loving,
and kind.

But you have chosen this fight.
And so have I.

So,
fellow warrior,
when you feel alone out here on the front lines,

when you feel like no one understands,
like no one truly cares.

Look to me,
fighting beside you,

and,
with a nod,

we will

ease
each other's
hurt.

Neighbor for a Week

I've moved into the suburbs,
your neighbor for the week.
I'm the man who sleeps in the van
you spotted down the street.

The Dodge that's parked beside the house,
boarded up and ivy-covered,
where I took a cold shower,
—no curtains, no power—
and each day I'll take another.

'Cause although I do not pay for a room,
I can't stand the feeling of grime,
offending eyes and attracting the flies,
being sticky all the time.

But even with my clean appearance,
you still don't smile or wave back.
When I'm walking the street and our eyes meet
and I flutter a friendly hand.

There's a distinctive glaze over your eyes,
something elusive you seek.
And I'd help you to find it,
if I just had the time,

but I'm only your neighbor for a week.

Over the Wall

It's a sleepless evening
and she visits me again.

Coming alive through one of many memories burnt deep into
my brain, recalled at will to fill lonely silences.

I'll take those memories with me to the grave,
those nights.
They are forever, and nothing can change that:

Nights when we searched each other to find ourselves,
perfect legs laid across mine as she told me how she believed
in nothing,
asking me what's the point of all this, of life.

Well,
I could tell her now that we were living it then, she and I.

I remember telling her that I didn't believe her nihilism.
I told her that she laughed like this meant something to her,
loved like it meant something.

I can still feel her now.
Kisses upon my bare chest,
lying silent and satisfied atop shifted sheets.
The look in her eyes as she turned her head,
meeting my gaze while we came together with fingers
intertwined.

Those were beautiful evenings, lost together,
And I wished they would last forever.

But then she built the wall.

Maybe it was always there,
but she had allowed me a brief peek beyond the brick,
revealing vast meadows and cerulean skies—

a massive, uncharted terrain,
enticing, enchanting,
begging to be explored.

Without a thought, I ran home,
gathered my things, and, with tail wagging,
returned to scale the wall.

But upon peeking over,
I found a wasteland:

Storm clouds vomiting black rain,
gnarled branches, growing from grey muck,
scratching the screaming sky.

Discouraged and confused,
I returned home and studied my map.
Perhaps I'd been lost?
Maybe a broken compass?
I checked my coordinates, reevaluated my equipment,
and set out once more,
determined and sure.
But again, after scaling the brick,
I found only desolate darkness,
miles of belching swamp and black mud.

Defeated,
I climbed down and sulked nine miles home.

Onward.

Days turned into weeks, and weeks into months.
A flower wilting, withering slowly.

I've since explored other spaces,
lived in different lands.
But, ever curious,
I still wander back to that wall now and again.

And each time I climb the cracked brick
to gaze upon an endless nothing,
a small part of me still holds the hope that,
one day,
I'll rise to relive that vibrant paradise.

Blue, green, and breathing life for miles
　　　　as it rolls without fear into the horizon.

They Keep it Cold

Here I am,
laid across the table.

Dissect me.

We're all students now,
social scientists gathering data.

Got your goggles?
Your white coat?

Good.

Break me down.
Categorize me.

Examine my face and file it with others like mine.

Make me into whatever you need me to be
to perpetuate your thoughts,
your feelings,
your beliefs.

Disregard my intention,
my desire to connect.

Throw them into the trash and wash your hands.
Watch the residue swirl down the drain.

Squeeze your fingers into rubber gloves
and make one long incision,
carefully removing the open mind.

Cut off a small sample,
and place it on a slide.

Label it.

Refer to your Facebook—I mean rulebook—for guidance.

"Let's see...
White,
    heterosexual,
        male...

Ah!
Chapter 6-B."

This system streamlines thought.

In such a busy world,
who really has time to treat every human as an individual?

Snap categorizations must be made.
Efficiency: a shining symptom of the new era.

So, back to the specimen.

Determine: male or female,
liberal or conservative,
gay or straight
(grey areas will be dealt with on a case-by-case basis).

Do you detect any misogynistic or feminist qualities?

Write these findings—
along with race, religion, and social class—
on a clear plastic container.
Then CAREFULLY place the sample inside
and close the airtight lid.

Containers will be stacked neatly on the proper shelves.

These are divided first by race,
then by religion,
and so forth.

Refer to the book for a full breakdown.

You'll find all shelves in the walk-in.
Careful. They keep it cold.

Don't forget to turn the lights off when you leave.

Little Things

Foraging for food with my siblings.

This particular kitchen expedition ended with the three of
us—aged nine, seven, and five—gathered around the dining
room table, splitting the spoils.

"A box of crackers!"

We opened the plastic package and excitedly grabbed a
Saltine each, bringing them quickly toward our mouths.
"Ew!" my little sister squeaked,
        throwing her cracker onto the table.
I studied my Saltine and was surprised to see it crawling with
moth larvae, burrowing tunnels through the tainted snack.

Though food was scarce at times,
there was always *something* to eat in the house.
Making a meal was often just a matter of getting creative.
There were times when we'd eat cereal twice a day—
with or without milk.
        Eggs and chopped hotdogs at 10 PM.
                Frozen pizza that would last us half the week.
Once, my sister stumbled upon a recipe I've yet to see
replicated beyond our circumstances:
the sugar and mustard sandwich.

Privy to our living situation, but unable to intervene,
our grandparents,
bless their hearts (as they would say in Mississippi drawls),
brought us bags of groceries.

They did this often
because most of Dad's money ended up feeding the folks who
worked at the nearby tavern.

When the groceries ran low,
my siblings and I had a backup plan:

Mining for change in the vents.

Each room in that house had at least one
HVAC vent in the floor.
My brother,
        sister,
                or myself
would remove a metal grate before lying on the carpet
to reach our little arm into the vent.

Then,
feeling around between protruding screws and dust bunnies,
we would rescue any coins that may have found their way
into the abyss.

Couch cushions and Dad's bed were also good places to find
stray change.

Once,
during a very successful scavenge,
we came upon three quarters in a kitchen drawer.
Seventy-five cents was enough to buy a soda from the
machine at the grocery store, a mile away.

It was a hot day,
and the three of us made the trek together,
debating flavors and anticipating the impending sugar-rush.

We agreed on black cherry.

Amidst a stuttering sniffle symphony (complete with muffled cough tubas), an eager eye sneaks a curious glance through the split fingers of an 8 AM face rub.

Morning commute on the 255.

The man's accompanying yawn unintentionally attracts the attention of the target: a female passenger who, until then, had been staring blankly at the metropolis passing outside her window. She meets the man's interested gaze, and the resulting synapse-shock sends eyes darting back to their previous positions with the force of a grenade detonated between the two.

Smartphone quick draw, back to safety.

The man opens recent text messages, frantically reading and rereading—appearing to have something very important beckoning his undivided.

She pulls a set of headphones from her purse and quickly inserts them into her ears, queuing a tune that floods her mind just in time to avoid any verbal interaction.

That was a close one.

The bus ride is long—45 minutes. Enough time for two episodes of "American Jerk-off" (commercial-free, of course). Every now and then, between desperate contestants shoving sharp objects into random orifices, the man and woman glance up from their screens to sneak peeks at each other (unaware that they are simultaneously watching the infamous "Cactus Episode"). But they're sure to look away from one another quickly; anything longer than a millisecond risks communication—an inconvenient interruption to such a sensational program.

Anxieties swell and shrink as frantic eyes scan the bus for substance, coming up empty and leaving hungry brains to devour memory scraps or daydream about leaping from some looming skyscraper.

But wait!
The screen.

Shiny hooks enter eyes, needles pierce eardrums, and an icepick shoots up each nostril
(effectively gouging the frontal lobe).

Ding!

Her stop.
The man looks to her, furtively,
Back to the phone.
Typing frantically as she passes.

A male of the human species must appear busy.
The provider, hunter-gatherer—
foraging for Facebook likes and right swipes.

Aha! He thinks. *Therein lies the answer.*

As the woman steps from the bus, the man moves to occupy her window seat—still warm—and peers outside while the 255 pulls away. He pauses the program—just as the host soaks a porcupine in KY jelly—and activates the camera function on his phone.

My god, she's gorgeous,
the man mumbles as he snaps a quick picture.
Black skirt on her way to work.

Just a quick enhancement...
And there it is!

Hunter indeed.

The male straightens his posture and scans the lifeless
passengers with a proud smile,
delighted he's captured a clear face shot
and one hell of a chance of tracking this girl down on the
latest dating app.

Jesus Rocks

The Muslim is singing.
Sweating, he leans forward,
mic stand in hand,
projecting passionate lyrics, backed by his band.

Rock and roll.
Leather jackets and denim vests.

There is no stage.
Just five musicians
sweating on a hardwood floor in front of forty onlookers.
Some of these spectators are also perspiring,
packed shoulder-to-shoulder,
tall cans in hand.

Swaying playfully to the beat,
swinging long hair when the music calls for it,
The Atheist bumps shoulders with The Christian.
The two share a smiling nod.
On the other side of the black-clad mass,
The Homophobe and The Lesbian bob their heads in unison.
One leans to the other,
speaking loudly to be heard over the crashing cymbals.
"This new guitar player is so good!"

The Policeman steps aside
so The Felon and her boyfriend can go out for a smoke.

At the bar,
The Conservative buys The Liberal a shot upon discovering
that they both own a copy of The Band's ultra-rare live
album.

No black and white here.
No red and blue.
Pro-lifers, gun enthusiasts.
None of that.

Just music.

Muhammad, Buddha, and Jesus are chatting at a table
toward the back of the room.
The Band's guitarist bursts into a raging solo,
and Jesus shoots his whiskey before standing up.
He speaks loudly to be heard over the crashing cymbals.
"'Scuse me, fellas, but I'll be right back."
Jesus removes his robe—
revealing The Band's black T-Shirt—
and drapes it over the back of his chair.

After wiping the hair from his face,
he pushes through the pulsating mass,
squeezing between two Jews on his way to the mosh pit.

Blank

Arnie Studebaker changed his name to Donnie Blank.
He thought it sounded edgier.

Donnie bought himself some clothes.
First, he got the hat that all the musicians wore.
Then he bought some jeans that looked a little dirty,
right off the shelf.

They were seventy-five dollars.

Arnie—I mean Donnie—didn't need glasses,
but he bought a pair and wore them anyway,
because that's what people did.

Donnie took several classes on songwriting
and had many books on the subject.
Twice a week he attended "Music Business Night School"
after working a job he hated, which offered comfortable pay.

Donnie saved up for the vintage guitar
with the beat-up tweed case—
the case that looked like it had been places, seen things.

Donnie went to a songwriter's group
every Thursday morning.
The group met at eight,
and Donnie felt good about meeting so early.
It made him feel serious about his craft.

Donnie told the group about his merchandise.
He had coffee mugs with his face on them.
He had T-shirts,
pencils,
dental floss,
cauliflower.
(Donnie didn't grow the vegetable, but he had applied a
sticker, adorned with his logo, to each head.)

Donnie Blank had a gig that week,
and he told everyone to come.
He posted fliers all over town—
in every shop window and on every telephone pole.

After a long day of promoting,
he bought a turkey sandwich and went home.
He sat down at his desk and pulled out a quill pen, some ink,
and a piece of paper.

Donnie Blank opened one of his songwriting books
and read for a moment before dipping the pen in ink.
Then he looked out the window,
watched the people live,

and had nothing to say.

She

She doesn't know I'm watching her,
sitting there beside the grass.

But I am.

She sits calmly,
waiting for me.

She always waits for me.

Knowing there's no rush, I soak in this image of her
through the branches of spring cedars.

I store this in my mind alongside other pictures I've collected
over the years.

Sitting in the high desert of Central Oregon
on a hot afternoon,
I strummed my guitar while she waved at passing semis
and gazed across the golden hills
        that seemed to roll on forever.

More than once
we slept together by the beach in San Francisco.

In Monterey Bay
we were woken at 4 AM by a filthy vagrant—
Charles Manson-esque—
who flapped his orange cape wildly in the night.

Startled, she and I grabbed our things and sped away.

We've cruised through the Cascades
more times than I can count,
following spontaneous whims that led us nowhere and
everywhere at once.

She is strong.
Reliable.
Loyal.

And she's mine.

Sometimes,

when the roar of the world gets too loud
and I feel as though my head may explode,
all I need to regain my sanity,

or as close to sanity as I can hope to experience,

is to hop inside her,
turn the key,
pick a song that we both love,

and speed down some lonesome road,

moving so fast that even my frantic thoughts can't catch up.

Santa Fe,
land of the adobe Starbucks.
A city where the self-proclaimed elite shop for culture to
decorate their empty walls.

An old couple, dressed to kill,
glittering, gaudy, and sipping their sixth margarita while
staring blankly at a live mariachi trio.

Not saying a word.
No applause.

Scoffing at the laughter of the table to their right.

A Peek at the Last Page

Please step back.
I don't want to hurt you.

Beauty,
while you were glowing, spilling your enchanting thoughts,
I played this story through to the end.

After the kisses, the wild nights,
afternoons by the river,
rushing waters shimmering in the sun,

after the love,
the laughs,
that time we danced in the bar
and they looked at us with strange disapproval,

when we recognized their underlying jealousy
and felt sorry for them,
because they would never know a happiness like ours,
a freedom like ours;

yes,
after all of this,
and more,

after we grew close,

just as I suspected,
I was bitten again
by the only demon I know,

and I left.

to find something.
to be alone,

again.

And it is strange because,
knowing this,
the inevitable conclusion of our compelling tale,
I ask myself why I still can't help but pull you close,
look into those intoxicating eyes,

and lose myself in the perfect woman that you are.

Written on the Steering Wheel, Speeding Through the Desert

Take me far from Vegas;
give me something real.
Feed me skies that I can taste and places that can heal.

Take your empty lap-dance eyes and drown them in a drink.
Fill your head with lights and sounds so you'll forget to think.

Crack the granite with your teeth,
thrusting your head into the sand,
and weep for your last dollar
when it's wrested from your hand.

Sell yourself on the boulevard to finance your next fix.
And when the tears stream down the mirror,
you can blame it on the tricks.

Because it's they—the eternal "they"—
who put you in this mess.
The tourists, your parents, the kids in the class,
the lover you hate, your ex.

So you drove on down to this awful town
to show the winner you can be,
but now it's spent scratch tickets and empty bottles
as far as the eye can see.

And you hear their laughter in your mind,
and it's burning in your guts.
And the man in black says, "Close your eyes,"
before he sews them shut.

Now you're running, screaming, frantic,
cutting flesh on broken glass.
And the wheel is spinning round and round,
whirling much too fast.

And if there was a God,
he'd show you the strength, the will and the way.

To care for yourself,
to be your own help,
to strain your tongue and say:

     Take me far from Vegas.
     Take me back to the start.
Where I'd already won
before the wheel had spun,

       and I knew this truth in my heart.

The Queen's Rest

Competition is fine.

As are the pursuits of one's deepest desires
and most coveted goals.

But, to this day,
few things make me feel more worthy as a man
than when a strong woman,
one who could move mountains with her graceful will
or bring a king to his knees with a well-chosen word,
removes her crown,
lays her head upon my chest,
and releases a heartfelt sigh,

allowing herself to slip away,

if only for a sweet moment.

Watch Your Step

They're out there,
coiled in the tall grass, ready to strike.
Ready to sink their fangs into you.
The con,
the hustle,
sucking from you that which they have failed to obtain.

They are despicable creatures.
But, perhaps, this is their calling,
their purpose.

Living landmines,
honing instincts and keeping senses sharp.

Watch your step.

One false move could easily cost you
an arm,
a leg,

or something more.

Chasing Carats

They wait in a single-file line
with glazed eyes,
screaming inside.

Suited on the surface to conceal lies,
and dreams that died the day they complied.

He buys

a shiny new car in an attempt to fill the void that
grows like a ravenous oil slick,
black and insatiable.

He spends every second chasing their symbols,
their ideals,
their prizes.

Some of these are rectangular and green,
good for trade or rolling into a straw,
allowing him to snort the American dream.

Other prizes have blonde hair, blue eyes,
silicone implants,
and Colgate smiles,
perfected through years of painstaking practice.

Though this facade may fool many,
a trained mind can still spot the madness behind the eyes,

burning hot coals that sear the inside of a plastic skull.

"Let me out!"
an unfamiliar voice cries.

The prize is startled by this voice,
and she orders another drink to drown the noise,
sucking voice and vodka through polished gums.

The drink washes the voice down,

down the esophagus,
further
into the stomach where it is trapped.

There
the vodka corners the voice,
smothers it.

The voice suffocates,
dies.

Then
there is only a warm and complacent silence.

The girl uses an issue of Cosmo
to wipe the sweat from her forehead,
leaving a streak of brown foundation
across the face of some photo-shopped idol.

"That was a close one,"
she says to nobody.

I Remember

We sat by the ocean
Staring into each other
And the world was perfect

It was as though nothing else existed

And now
Without you

Nothing will

The Fire

I told her I'm sometimes scared of people,
scared of talking to them.

I told her I feel each interaction deeply,
that they affect me tremendously.

She wanted to understand better,
so I told her about the fire.

The fire in her.
      The fire in me.

The fire that blazes out of the eyes,
across time and space,
from another soul to mine.

I told her that I can feel its heat,
      its intensity,
      every time.

Behind every word I see a thousand thoughts,
hidden within each nervous twitch,
      poorly concealed by forced smiles.

The thoughts scream at me:
Insecurity
      Greed
          Lies!

Often, I hear these origins of intention
rather than the words spoken.

On the other hand, when the radiant speak I feel love.
I feel playfulness,
      innocence and caring,
          compassion.

I can spot true beauty though the thickest mask.

At least I think I can.

This may be a delusion,
this supposed social intuition.
But time and again,
it has proven itself true.

After hearing all of this,
She looked deep into me and nodded
        understandingly.

But there was a shade of doubt on her face.

Or maybe there wasn't.

Dirty Work

Beyond music

I usually have a side job.

Clocking these extra hours fattens the wallet,
adding some padding for the
ever-looming financial gut-punch
(You know, the right hook that
hits hardest when you're flying highest.)

The brakes go out.
The bills show up.

Of the many jobs I've had, I prefer work that leaves me dirty,
scrubbing my grimy arms up to the shoulder.

I want steel splinters burnt into my skin.
Dust in the lungs.

Hack it up.
Spit out the day.

I want to prick my fingers on a pocketful of nails as I'm
digging for change. I want to learn new curse words in
Spanish while dangling from freshly cut rafters.

I want danger,
the potential for pain.
Hammer-smashed fingers and nails through the boots,
splinters in the eye because I forgot to put my sunglasses on.
The Skilsaw spits and calls me a dumbass.
Teaches me.
Makes me stronger.

I want to scratch my fiberglass itch.
Throw away my clothes.

I want the much-anticipated hot shower to feel
like a ten-minute orgasm.
I want to strut through the hordes of soft bodies
and uncalloused hands
      knowing I can,
           knowing I did,
knowing that everywhere I could possibly hope to go,
there is a job for someone who's willing to sweat.

Someone who's willing to do the dirty work.

Elsewhere

Words fall short.
Moments sail past without brushing my shoulder.
Because I'm not here;
I'm in my head.

Imagining somewhere else while you sit there,
looking beautiful.
And everything that matters
slips like sand through my fingers.

Little Boy Blue

It's your birthday today,
and I'm listening to Neil Young.

I don't know if you can listen to music where you are,
but if you can't, then you may never hear Neil Young again.

I don't know much about you,
because you didn't know much about you.

But I think you would've liked this song.

A nice beat, thumping bass,
steel guitar and thoughtful lyrics.

I remember once you asked me to mail you the lyrics to
"Cat's in the Cradle" by Harry Chapin.
You liked that song,
the one about the father and son
who always planned to connect,
but never quite got around to it.

In your honor,
I'll listen to it now.

Sorry, Neil.

I've found the song, pressed play, and the music has begun.
(Strange trying to focus on the words coming into my head
while others leave through the fingers.)
I'm just going to listen for a while...

This has been written to show that

Time
Is
Passing

When you comin' home dad?
I don't know when.
But we'll be together then, son
You know we'll have a good time then.

More
Time
Passing

Another chorus,

A memory:

Me, crying,
running to the neighbor's house in the middle of the night,
dressed only in one of your long, sweat-stained undershirts.

The police waited with us until you came home.

The song's tempo slows, and the last chord rings out.

Now, I don't have much to say.
And you can't say anything, either,
because you're not here.

Just like old times.

Tough to Type when One's Fingers are Crossed

Sometimes I feel worthless,
like this is all a joke.

Sitting here on the couch, feet up on the coffee table,
typing away and watching words crawl across the screen.
Words that have found their way to you.

Hello.

It takes some degree of delusion to believe that one has
written something worth reading,
and another madness to actually share it.
So I sometimes wonder if that's all this is:
Delusion.
Madness.

Sitting here, talking to myself,
wasting days and nights.
Driven by some desire I'll never understand.

Hoping...

Hoping that these words will do something.
Mean something.

To me.
To you.

And if they don't,
well,
I suppose I have no choice in that matter.

All I can do is listen,
and oblige when these thoughts beg me to set them free.

<u>Boom!</u>

A bomb went off.
The streets were closed.

And,
for the first time
in my two months living in this neighborhood,
people sat outside on the grass.

Talking.

Clocking in

Today my coworkers are a choir of chatty birds,
      chirping back and forth,
            catching up in early spring.

Much to talk about after many months of winter vacation.

They must speak loudly to be heard over the nearby creek,
equally exuberant as it rushes purposefully
toward Puget Sound.

The chair I'm seated on isn't the standard-issue office throne,
with the wheels and
little lever used to raise or lower the seat.

Crank it all the way up,
then spin in a circle,
      pulling the lever as you whip around,
          descending clockwise,
          slowly.

No,
I'm sitting on a log.
A fallen comrade of these cherry blossoms that surround me.
      They are blooming beautifully, feeding bees.

No ceiling.
No mineral fiber tiles or buzzing fluorescent bulbs.

      Azure sky.
      The loving sun warming my winter-whitened skin.

No carpet.
No headache odor of overnight chemical cleanings.

      The grass is wet with morning dew;
      each tiny droplet shimmers,
      a rainbow jewel in the early light.

Between the blades
there are golden dandelions,
white daisies.

Solitude.
Except for that fat black bee,
my supervisor.

He smells my shoe,
        realizes he cannot pollinate it,
            and moves on.

Written at a Bar in Smoke Lake City

I can't shake the feeling that we're circling the drain,
so I'll take another drink and hope it numbs the pain.

A toast to the forests on fire in the west.
Cold beer to wash away this smoky breath.

You speak about the future, but I don't know if we'll see it.
You've got a five-year plan,
and I'm praying we see the weekend.

Right now it seems so hopeless, like we've gone in too deep.
So if I can't wake from this nightmare,

then I'll put myself to sleep.

<u>Note to Self</u>

Tell them you love them
While they are still alive

They won't be around to hear their eulogies

The Lovers

They sat in silence and drank the wine, blinking occasionally.
With each labored breath, the strong bodies they had once
inhabited cried out from beneath heavy layers of fat.
"Good wine," Carol said.
Mike held his glass in front of his face,
considering the cabernet as he swished it around.
"Yup," he replied.
The lowering of his glass revealed the waitress, at the bar
across the room.
Mike stared as the girl stood on her tiptoes to reach a bottle
from the high shelf.
As the waitress extended an arm, her shirt lifted,
revealing the small of her back.
It was muscular and smooth, with two little dimples like
smiling eyes, just above the belt line.
Mike set his glass on the mahogany table beside him.
Then he fidgeted with his wedding ring.

Flames roared on the hearth, and an old blues musician
crooned through the ceiling-mounted speakers.
Other than the occasional bend of a soulful guitar string,
or the fire's erratic crackle,

the tasting room was silent.

Carol took another sip of the wine
and glanced toward the wall.
A painting of Venice hung inside an ornate golden frame.

The image featured two young lovers, seated in a gondola.
The boat's pilot stood proudly atop the stern,
guiding the couple through the city's watery streets.
The watercolor man and watercolor woman sat facing one
another—smiling brightly and staring lovingly—their
foreheads pressed tightly together, fingers interlocked.
Whatever the brush-stroke beau had said to his lady,
it was causing her to blush.

"What are you looking at?" Mike asked,
shattering Carol's trance.

After a contemplative sigh,
Carol surveyed the lifeless room.
She looked at her wine.

The blues man sang,

and the fire went pip-pop.

Hunting Monsters

I cried today,
but then I stopped myself.
because that's what you would have told me to do.

I shouldn't have gone through your things,
should have known that it would stir something.
But grandma was going to be staying in your old room,
and those boxes were too heavy for her to lift on her own.

I stacked them near the closet,
one by one,
Sneaking peeks under cardboards flaps—
glimpses into manila envelopes,
glimpses into your mind.

Conspiracy theories, secret plots,
letters to senators—hundreds of them,
all neatly filed, logged, and labeled.

All very well written.

I couldn't help but wonder where this marriage of
talent and tenacity would have taken you,
had you chosen to live differently.

Breathing deeply,
I glanced from one of your
beautifully streamlined chem-trail ramblings
toward a secondhand dresser
decorated with a myriad of multicolored stickers,
trying to imagine the teenager who'd owned it before you.

An American flag sat atop that dresser,
folded into a neat triangle.

Beside the flag,
a black-and-white picture of you and your brothers lay

covered by a thin layer of dust.

You were all young, wearing white T-shirts.

I blew dust from the glass and stood the frame upright,
contemplating the lives of three men I never knew.

I bet you miss your brothers;
you all looked so happy in that picture.

Maybe that's why you did it?
An attempt to fill some sibling-sized void?

There's a good chance I'll never know.

But, staring at that dresser,
I began to think that maybe you'd left me some clues.

I slid open the top drawer,
Hoping to find madness—
something to help it all make sense.

Instead, I found myself.

A videocassette of a concert I'd played as a teenager
beside a CD I'd made you as a birthday gift,
loaded with songs that we both loved.

I yanked open the second drawer,
revealing random writings and a cache of books:
Last of the Mohicans,
H.G. Wells,
nothing out of the ordinary.

Surely the third drawer would contain the smoking gun,
something sick and twisted.
I opened it with an exuberant anticipation
that instantly evaporated.

Movies.
An entire drawer full of movies.
Mostly comedies,
the ones you and I watched together while I was growing up.

Defeated, I sat down on the bed,
hands dangling between my legs.

I'd opened those drawers looking for a monster,
some evidence that would explain your perverse ways.

Instead,
I found something even more terrifying.

I found a man.

Sitting Contradiction

When I'm here—and only here—it's nice.

However.
Fabricated futures,
labels,
the idea of forever:
these things make me uncomfortable.

I'm reflecting on a hopeful future of the past
that never came to be:
Standing on stage
in front of seventy thousand screaming fans.
Playing a show and then hopping on a bus,
headed toward the next town.

This fantasy—this ambition of yesterday—
somehow no longer appeals.
This routine, this schedule.

On stage or not, though, I must share my music.
It is written.
And if it is recorded, it will be alive.
Forever.
(Maybe not such a scary word, after all.)

Strangely, for some reason,
in my well-conditioned mind,
the creation and sharing of art doesn't seem enough.
Worldwide reverence seems necessary
to validate my efforts.

What a twisted mirage.

Goddamned *American Idol.*

The real art is this life, the day-to-day.
This is the show. Each moment.

Inhale experience. Exhale creation.
Share.

I've always done this.
I just need to keep moving forward, staying true to myself.
Right now the thing that seems to excite me the most is *this*.
Writing.

It has always been there, burning since I was young.

I did it at Grandma's house on small scraps of paper.
In grade school—stories about aliens and monsters.
In high school it was the only subject I ever enjoyed.

The blank page is my canvas,
and these words are my paint.

Splish.
Splash.

I love it.

Sitting here in the dark,
savoring the comfort of the nest,

and, between satisfied breaths,
        fantasizing about where I'll go once the lease is up.

The Balloon and the Brick

I tried to fly, but you were weighing me down.
Bound together, we never left the ground.

For a while I was content to enjoy the scene,
but curiosity soon got the best of me.

      I imagined what life was like just over the hills,
      but the idea of flying made you ill.

I cried when I realized what I'd need to do.
and while you were sleeping, I cut myself loose.

I'm writing you now to describe a breathtaking scene,
as I'm floating over mountains and rivers and trees.

Yes, sometimes it hurts,
because I miss you still,

      but the idea of flying made you ill.

*

It was dark when I woke up.

Middle of the night;
my stomach felt strange.
I sat up—looking through my open door, into the hallway—
and saw the ghost of an old woman
walking toward my room.

She wasn't really there, though,
and somehow I knew you weren't, either.

Your room was empty.
I could feel it.

Slowly, I stepped barefoot onto the carpet,
crept into the hallway,
making sure not to wake my little brother.

The house was quiet.
Your door was cracked.

A peek inside your room confirmed my suspicions:

The bed was vacant.
And, for some reason,

I was relieved.

Where the Truth Lies

Monica dusts her cheeks with rouge;
it helps her feel beautiful.
She coats her lips with vermillion wax,
making them full and inviting.
Her best girlfriend styles her hair,
pulling it up tight, a discreet black bun.
Monica dresses herself in the finest silk,
ornate patterns, designed to turn heads
and generate jealous whispers.

But,
despite the elaborate presentation,
Monica cannot hide her eyes,
decorated with thick liner and perfectly applied mascara—
eyes that scream of every infidelity,
every lie.
Icy windows allowing me a glimpse into that lonely soul.

There
I see a little girl clawing desperately at the rusted bars of a
self-constructed cage.
Red flakes stick to her hand,
smearing across her cheek as she wipes away the tears.

Like a stray dog on a cold night
she whimpers,
she begs.
"Love me!"

But, shaking my head, I must turn away

 and hope she finds the key that dangles from her neck.

A Fine Reward

A calloused handshake tells a thousand tales;
stories of split wood, broken concrete,
and shoveled trenches.

Sweat and blood,
cursing and headache,
pain and glory.

Hallelujah.

A cold beer after a hard day,
moving the mile-marker.
Raising the bar,
expanding the awareness of one's own ability.

What a challenging opportunity that arises from the ashes of
a sleepless night!
When a heavy hammer is raised by a weary hand,
and the voice within barks something about honoring
a commitment.

The reward for pulling the weight,
for passing the test,
cannot be measured by conventional means.

The prize is the ability to,
in the midst of the aforementioned handshake,
match your partner's grip with confidence,

and look them comfortably in the eye.

Flies and Mexican Wrestlers on the Wall

I sat there and drew a deep breath.
Then I took another drink
and wondered what the hell I was doing there

in the basement of some bar.

     1 AM
     Chattering tables
     Everything strange, bathed in red light

Sombreros hanging from the ceiling
and Lucha Libres on the walls,
staring at me through painted eyes.

I wanted something.
I think.

There was a table full of girls ahead of me.
Four of them,
     one guy.
Another dude sat down.
Four of them,
     two guys.

I knew I was supposed to go over there,
talk to the girls,
try to make something happen.
    "Hey, I'm Alex."
        "Hi, I'm (insert name here)."
    "What do you do?"
       "Where did you grow up?"
       "Where do you live?"
         "Do you like panda bears?"

      "Wouldn't it be strange
         if our ears were on our feet?"

I glanced to my right.
A fellow twenty-something sat atop the backrest of his booth,
scanning the room like a lifeguard.

He and I were of the same mindset,
sitting on the sidelines, studying the scene,
And I thought about saying something to him about this,

but then I didn't.

Eyes Don't Grow

Orsi tells me that your eyes don't grow.
They're the same size when you're forty as when you're
pooping in diapers.
I don't know if I believe her, but it's an interesting thought.

I'm now picturing her as a little, blonde, Hungarian baby.
I can see it clearly:
Tiny green eyes and a wide smile,
illuminating any room her proud parents parade her
through.

Orsi licks her lips—subtly,
probably doesn't even notice that she's doing it.
I've been looking at her for a while now,
but she doesn't seem to mind.
There's no insecurity on her face—
no discomfort—
just a confident ease, radiating across our little table
and doing funny things to my stomach.

I glance out the window.
Mist from the waterfall's relentless rush
ascends like a plume of smoke from the steep cliffs.
My eyes trace the vapor as it rises.

In the background, the sunlight—
fighting fiercely against an inevitable descent—
punches scattered holes through tattered clouds.

That sun has been a great companion to Orsi and me,
hiking all day with us through evergreen hills.

I am sad to see it go.

The setting star is a subtle reminder of the short time that
the two of us have together.
Orsi leaves in the morning, back to Dubai,

where she will be reunited with her three dogs
and give her godson a bulging bag of stateside gifts.

Something about this nagging deadline, this certainty,
begs me to drink every detail with a slow savor:
Emerald eyes, vibrant smile, caramel skin, golden hair—
the way she looks down at the table and bites her lip
after I'm able to make her laugh—
the waterfall, tangerine sky, the mist, this beer...

Right back to those eyes.

Orsi told me that your eyes don't grow.
They're the same size when you're forty as when you're
pooping in diapers.
I don't know if I believe her, but it's an interesting thought.

Cowboy in a Seattle Bar

He walks across the room, slowly.

Not because he's going anywhere,
but because he wants someone to notice.

Broken One

Allan was hit by a car in Fredericksburg, Texas,
killed instantly.

He is survived by a plethora of Facebook likes
and YouTube views,
accumulated over the years as he posted video after video
of him harassing random strangers.

"Go fuck yourself!"
he would yell at unsuspecting passerby,
pointing his phone at them
to film their often irate reactions.

These videos garnered many "thumbs-ups"
and laughing-face icons,
none of which attended his funeral.

Allan's girlfriend,
of whom he would post videos,
asking her condescending questions and
mocking her lack of intelligence,

she attended the service,
but was unable to feel grief.

Allan's girlfriend felt guilty about her stoic state;
felt like there was something wrong with her.
This is what Allan would have told her.

She was always
        the broken one.

Allan would have told her she was strange
in the most entertaining fashion,
and he would have filmed it.
Shared it.

Internet spectators would've laughed collectively
from the darkness of lonely rooms.
And Allan would feel the dopamine rush of
a thousand "Likes"
while his girlfriend would sob
and beg him to remove the clip.

Allan would lie,
say he would delete the video,
but never get around to it.

Realizing this,
remembering this,
Allan's girlfriend felt her face fill with blood,
bile creeping up the esophagus.

She felt an almost uncontrollable urge to
          slap that lifeless face,
still wearing his trademark shit-eating smirk.

Instead of doing this
in the middle of Mom's sniffling, red-eyed eulogy,

Allan's girlfriend stood up
and left without saying goodbye.

Pull

I loved you
because I'd learned to love pain:
the struggle of performing for you,
begging for the approval that—
even if you were capable of giving—
I could never fully accept.

Because in my mind,
I wasn't worthy.

It was interesting seeing you today
because I recognized that
the more I love myself,
the less I feel the need to be
in your presence.

Lifting you up gave me purpose,
a sense of worth
I would not give myself.

But now,
after months of lifting me—
and only me—
I see
that holding my own weight
is enough to keep me strong.

And I know now that the only way
any of us can build muscle
is by pulling
ourselves
up.

No one can do it for us.

So I'll no longer be giving you the boost.

I will also say this:
Your problems are not alcohol's fault.
They are not God's fault.
The condition did not cause them,
and neither did I
or he
or she.

You
and the choices you've made
created your circumstances.

And
as I must live with my sometimes stupid choices,
you must learn to accept yours.

Pull.
Harder.

You can do it.

You
are
strong
enough.

Beast

This beast eats miles.
Unknown stretches of mountain highway
and wide-skied desert rides.

It craves danger, excitement,
proof of life.

The beast feeds on stories, laughter,
tears.

It wants to know everything,
feel everything, be everything,

touch everybody.

It needs to
        move.

It needs to
        love.

And then it needs to lose.

The beast in me has lived and died a thousand times,
growing stronger with each rebirth.

I cannot escape it. I cannot ignore it.

I can only feed it
and marvel at the many gifts it gives

    to me.

And, maybe,

      to you.

*

There is a stillness here,
the funk of fertile earth.

The first petals of spring falling to the ground
where they will be trampled by eager lovers,
sneaking through the trees to catch the perfect moment:

this one.

From Muse to Me

You are going to be tired,
and you will need to decide
if sleep is more important than your dream.

You are going to be in pain,
and you will need to decide which weighs more:
your suffering or your goals.

You are going to be scared,
but you will need to look fear in the eye,
buy it a drink,
and make it a friend.

The two of you will be riding together until the very end.

You will have doubt.
Look this monster in the eye as well,
then spit in its face with every ounce of grit you've got.

Shove the beast onto its back,
and take a step
over its trembling body,
onward.

There will always be something calling you,
beckoning.
Some event or activity,
someone who needs your attention,
your energy.

Do not shut these people or experiences out,
but choose wisely the ways that you spend your time.
Precious currency.

For, once this is spent,
there is no refund.

Along this road
many forces will conspire to break you,
and it is your choice whether or not you give them
permission to do so.

Your choice:
Shine bright with your unique light
or allow the inevitable darkness
to swallow you whole.

Buenas Tardes

Spider web power lines,
wrapped in a tangled mess around an upright, rotting log.
An urban rooster screams in the distance.
Moss-ravaged clay shingles line corrugated roofs.

An expressionless man sits atop a gas tanker as it lumbers up
a steep cobblestone incline.

Hiking up the broken concrete stairs,
I glance toward the flat roof on my right and lock eyes with a
husky pup, lying on his side and panting in a patch of
afternoon sun.
*Maybe he's tired from chasing one of Puerto Vallarta's
many stray* gatos?

Swarms of yellow jacket taxi cabs,
zipping and buzzing through tight alleyways.
"You want a ride, *amigo*?"

"Sure, take me anywhere but the boardwalk,
the gringo habitat.
I didn't come to Mexico to eat cheeseburgers and listen to
classic rock cover bands."

A dirt bike whizzes past, its pilot yelling into a cell phone.
There's a taco stand on every block,
plastic chairs warmed by local asses as folks devour spicy
morsels and share stories about their day.

Wow, look at that church.

"I'll get out here."
"Hundred pesos."
"*Gracias.*"

Huge double doors open wide,
the Holy Father's welcoming embrace.

In my head, I hear his heavenly voice.
"Marvel at my golden monuments,
my polished marble altars.
Look upward, my son.
Behold the hope that radiates through
kaleidoscope stained glass."

This temple is open to the public, yet there is no graffiti.
No vandalism.
No security guard.

No need.

Here in Mexico—
at least in this area—
there is civility, respect.

I spend a moment with eyes closed,
basking in the majesty of the monstrous structure.

       After this moment, I move along.

Time to meet with a few friends on the beach.
A bucket of beer costs five dollars.
We sip the cold brew and watch a boogie boarder ride
massive breakers on his stomach,
gliding across the water like a penguin in swim trunks.

Eighty degrees in January.

"*Amigo!*"
A man, wearing white clothes, sandals, and a large straw hat,
shows me an open briefcase lined with silver jewelry.
"*Estoy bien, gracias.*"

We order fresh guacamole, squeeze the lime over it.
Such a sweet scent.
Quesadillas are packed with fresh shrimp that pop between
your teeth.

Even the tortilla chips taste better down here.

On the sand, two women pull their dresses up to their knees
and run—giggling—to escape the rapidly approaching ocean.

I could stay here forever.

"You guys want a ride out to Yelapa Island?"

We five look at each other.

"*Si.*"

We buy a case of Corona and follow our guide to the end of a
long dock where he waves to one of many boats bobbing up
and down in the lazy wake.
The pilot starts his engine and
edges an old pile-of-floating-shit up against the pier.
The boat smells like gasoline.

A sluggish pelican takes a half-assed snap at my buddy's
hand, which he'd been waving in front of the bird's face.

Our group pays the man and hops into the little zipper.
For the next hour we
bounce across the waves at a steady pace.
With each bump,
Puerto Vallarta gets smaller and the beers get emptier.

Our pilot, Carlos, stands at the back of the boat,
wearing what seems to be the standard local uniform:
White slacks, white button-up shirt, sandals, and a straw hat.
He knows only enough English to handle business, and
spends the entire boat ride focused intently on
the water ahead.

There's a pod of dolphins,
glistening as they arc gracefully across the water.
        A floating coconut, bobbing with the tide.

Boom!

"What was that, Carlos?"
        "Sea turtle."

Yelapa Island.
A little cove cradled by jungle.
There are a few houses up on the hillside with
lawn-chair-lined decks perched proudly above the palms.
Carlos kills the engine and lets the waves push us toward
shore.
Once the hull is resting safely on the sand,
we jump into the water
        quickly,
before the tide sucks the boat back out to sea.

"Welcome, *amigos!*"

We are instantly greeted,
seated beneath a giant straw umbrella,
and presented with five shots of *raicilla*,
Mexican moonshine.
Something to lubricate the wallets.

"*Salud!*"

The translucent juice burns like rubbing alcohol.
It clears my sinuses and brings tears to my eyes.
As I'm regaining my senses,
a little dog lifts his leg to piss on a cinder block wall.
The dog kicks the sand twice before scampering beneath a
table full of local guys who are smoking and playing poker.

"Picture with Pedro?"
A man begins to set a massive iguana onto my buddy's
shoulder.
My buddy stands up—laughing—
and politely sends the man and Pedro on their way.

We decide to lay in the sun.
As our group stands from the table,
we notice that Carlos has found a lawn chair and is lounging,
snoring beneath his straw hat.

We find lawn chairs of our own,
stretch out and soak up solar tingles.
When our Seattle blood gets too hot, we cool off in the ocean,
floating on our backs and feeling the time disappear.

Eighty degrees in January.
I could stay here forever.

After a sun-soaked eternity, Carlos shuffles across the sand,
wiping sleep from his eyes.

Time to go back to Puerto.

      Bumping across the water.

We dock and step from the wobbly boat.
"*Gracias*, Carlos!"
We tip him a few hundred pesos.
He smiles.

As we walk along the beach,
on our way to whatever comes next,
I take a deep breath and feel the life surge through my body.
What an amazing paradise this is.

What a spectacular reality.

After a few more sandy steps,
a sweet senorita crosses my path.
She looks into me.
Long, healthy black locks,
bare brown feet.

Thick hips sway with each step.

"Hola," I say.
The girl instantly flashes a bright smile.
"Buenas tardes."

Yes,
I think to myself.

Yes, it is.

A huge thank you to editors Anna Eklund and Sarah Pasillas. Your hard work polished and streamlined this collection.

I'm also grateful for the feedback of Ben and Megan Rouse, Iris Chamberlain, Becky Zuckerberg, Amanda Garcia, and Brittney Townsend.
Your insight and perspective were invaluable.

Cover art by Ashley Zuckerberg.
Instagram: @fromatozcrafts

Graphic design by Mario Di Sandro.
www.mariodisandro.com

Photo by: Quan Ho – *Instagram: @quanhoanho101*

For more from Alex Rasmussen, visit
www.alexrasmusic.com

Find Alex Rasmussen on Spotify, iTunes,
and all other streaming platforms.

@alexrasmusic on Instagram, Facebook.

Made in the USA
Monee, IL
26 June 2023